Management Consulting for Medics

By

Dr. Aroon Baskaradas

Copyright

Management Consulting for Medics

Copyright © Eurekadoc Publishing, 2016

Publisher

Eurekadoc Publishing
Kemp House, 152 City Road, London, EC1V 2NX
Web: www.eurekadoc.com
Email: info@eurekadocpublishing.com
Tel: 0203 289 1311

Disclaimer

Contents

Introduction

The pilot threw the doors open and I jumped out of the chopper. The whirling rotor blades still spinning in a frenzy even though they had started to slow down. I looked over the edge and saw the whole of New York City sprawled out before me. We had landed on one of the city's tallest skyscrapers. I glanced at my Breitling. I was right on time for the presentation. I buttoned up my sharp Italian suit and grabbed the black briefcase that was handed to me. The waiting aides whisked me off to the boardroom. Once pleasantries were out of the way, I turned to address the eager audience. Slowly and meticulously, I told them everything – the analytics, the failures of management. I unraveled the truth and began to deconstruct their organisation, piece by piece. They listened as if pearls were coming out of my mouth. Man ... I loved consulting.

To some people, consulting is often thought of as a high flying, glamorous and well paid, although cut-throat, job. In my experience, it is interesting to note that only one of those is consistently true. It's not particularly high flying – I've never once been in a helicopter and my suits are not made in Italy. Also, consulting is not always glamorous, particularly in the health sector, though we do have some great Christmas parties. It's not too cut-throat either, which may surprise you but it is however, fairly well paid, intellectually stimulating and a rewarding career for individuals with a talent for business and strategy.

Let me tell you about my story and how I got into consulting, but let me also give you a warts-and-all opinion of the journey, so you can see if it's right for you. In this book, I will advise you on how you can get into consulting, with the potential to enjoy a better quality of life.

My Story

Like everyone else on the conveyor belt, I left medical school starry-eyed, and my main concern was wondering how best to wear my stethoscope and which holiday destination to go to with my very first paycheck and annual leave – that, and not wanting to cause any patient fatalities. I was among the second cohort of the very first 'foundation year' doctors. The FY2s above me were the first FY2s ever, and I was a brand spanking new FY1.

I had some fantastic house jobs in a teaching hospital and a district general – and others that were not so great. You took the crazy-busy jobs on the chin because you felt a massive sense of responsibility to your patients and knew that this grueling time would pass as you became more senior (or so you thought!).

The busy jobs weren't necessarily the worst if you felt part of the team, valued and respected by your seniors. On the other hand, the jobs where you were the only ward doctor and your seniors had vanished off the face of the planet (usually surgical jobs sadly) were the soul-destroying ones.

After moving onto an orthopaedic training program and reaching the registrar level, I began to notice a most peculiar trend: very good surgical trainees who were in the process of gaining their CCTs were having to do fellowship after fellowship before finding a decent consultant post because competition was too high. How could this be right after six years of medical school, two years of foundation program and seven to eight years of specialty training, with the result of then finding no job to go to? I didn't fit the orthopaedic stereotype, so how would I get that elusive consultant post?

How could I make myself stand out? Well, I noticed that those getting jobs had all done PhDs or MDs and committed numerous years to research. It seemed as though the system wanted clinicians who could demonstrate that they were active in research. But what if you weren't interested in research? Why would you stop doing what you love (clinical work and operating) to do something that you didn't have a true interest in? At this point, I looked further afield and found my calling in management consulting. I thought it would be a great advantage to have an understanding of how health systems are run, so that I could bring this knowledge back to the NHS. It was then that I decided to do an MBA and begin my research into consulting. I believed that a career in it would complement my MBA, not to mention provide a unique insight into the world of healthcare management. The rest, as they say, is history, and I am now a living and breathing surgical trainee turned management consultant.

Having been through the journey, I am confident that every one of you can do it. A career in consulting is definitely within reach.

Let me show you how ...

Chapter 1

Why become a management consultant?

Making a career change is an important process and one that requires a lot of thought. Let's explore some of the reasons why you may wish to move into management consultancy.

1. We have the right skills

As a medic, you have **amazing** talents. You have the ability to walk into any place, anywhere in the world, pick any person, build instant rapport, put them at ease and discuss detailed facts about their life and very personal issues within about 30 seconds of meeting them. To management consultant firms, this is gold dust.

Not only that, you are intelligent, academically unmatched, creative, emotionally rock solid (usually), curious and can cut down complex problems into tiny little chunks that you can chomp up for breakfast with no sleep and without even batting an eyelid.

You are a machine! Who wouldn't want you?

On top of these attributes, we have gained so much experience leading teams, communicating, discussing, debating and persuading. You may not realise it, but all those radiology requests that you had to barter for, have actually given you some added value. Even better still, for those who want to go into the healthcare sector, we know hospitals. We know them like no one else does.

All of our skills are completely **transferable**, and if you think about what it really means to be a management consultant, it's no wonder that it's a natural career option for us.

2. The variety

You will **never** work the same day twice as a consultant, and you will always spend it with a variety of different colleagues on an array of different projects.

In terms of the people you will encounter, they will come from diverse backgrounds and it will be quite refreshing to learn from them, as they bring their own unique viewpoints. Their approach to things will immensely add to your frame of reference. You will also get regular contact and exposure to senior decision makers, which is something that doesn't usually happen until quite late in other careers.

In terms of the work itself, projects can be challenging and dynamic. You get to use your brain and creativity rather than working on autopilot all day long. Projects can last anywhere from a few days to a few months, and each and every one is unique. Most projects follow a clear structure with an initial phase of diagnosing client problems, followed by carrying out investigations or data gathering, and then an analysis phase resulting in a final solution design or 'implementation planning' (note the parallels with medicine).

Other projects can be less structured; for example, you may be asked to solve a particular challenge for a client or even manage a large-scale change, such as a merger between two healthcare trusts or the acquisition of a new service or site by an existing organisation.

Think of any problem you have seen in the NHS organisations you have worked for – there has probably been a role for consultancy to play in solving it.

3. Personal and professional development

Imagine working in an environment where every day you grow and develop as a person and as a business-focused leader. Imagine an organisation that sets aside time, money and senior-level people to ensure that you get the support, mentoring and education to do your job properly and excel as an individual. This is what the setup for personal and professional development in management consultancy firms is like. It is phenomenal!

You will become an expert at analysing trends, asking the right questions and writing business cases or preparing proposals. Material for clients has to be perfect and you become accustomed to scrutinising things with a fine-toothed comb.

Your presentation skills (which after years of doing clinical presentations should be pretty good already) will be honed on a daily basis, and you will get used to picking up conversations with senior decision makers with ease.

At the very least, you will develop the ability to 'think big', whilst simultaneously focussing on the details that really enhance the big picture. By 'thinking big', you will gain a strong appreciation for the world beyond medicine, learn about the networks in healthcare or business, and learn to think strategically, not only about your organisation but also about others in the market and how to compete with them.

Your thought processes will shift from being focused around individual patients and the treatment that they require to a more all-encompassing view of wider health economies. You will be thinking about 'Where is this organisation going?', 'How can we future proof it or compete?' or 'How can we do our best for this entire cohort of people?'.

4. Job satisfaction

Using your existing knowledge coupled with the new skills you learn in consulting to bring about large-scale transformation can be a very rewarding process.

We often work right at the heart of organisations, in their executive suites with their CEOs and CFOs (chief financial officers – yes, one of the many acronyms I had to look up when I first got into consulting), tackling their biggest issues. It is a very privileged place to be and a side of the organisation that many of their own employees can only dream of becoming involved in.

Seeing groups of people who would not normally get on with each other, come together and create brilliant plans for the future, all at your request and with your patience and encouragement, is a very humbling experience. An example of this was when I was leading a work stream on the merger process of two hospitals. Two, previously rival, departments were refusing to co-operate but when I spelled out the financial consequences of them not coming together and highlighted the threat of the loss of jobs and services for patients, this galvanised them into action. They were able to put aside their differences and work together towards a common goal. At the end of the process, they appreciated my openessess, ability to listen, manage their conflict and steer them in the right direction. This is consulting at it's best.

Above all, the satisfaction of winning a project or completing one successfully through teamwork and diligence keeps you going as a management consultant.

5. The team culture & your colleagues

Are you a creative person? Are you an innovative person? Perhaps those aren't your strengths, and you need someone with those talents to inspire you. Or, perhaps, you are good at problem solving but need someone with analytical skills to support you.

The breadth of skills and mix of minds that you will encounter in a consultancy firm can be mind-blowing. You never have to go far to find someone who has achieved great things in their life and is now reinvesting their energy and ideas in you, your team and the client.

I've never had my thoughts challenged on a daily basis as much as I have had in a management consultancy firm. People will pick apart what you say and make you think about problems from new perspectives. They will challenge your ideas and preconceptions in such a way that sometimes you will be stretched, though rarely made uncomfortable, and you will always be in a position to learn from your colleagues.

The ways in which you work with your team will also be quite refreshing: meetings, brainstorming sessions, discussion lunches, breakfast meets, workshops – the list goes on. In consultancy, unlike the banking sector or some corporate sectors, the culture is one of collaboration and working together effectively.

6. The travel

The world of consulting is big. In fact, it's so big that it makes the real world feel smaller. Clients can be based all over the country, and you will regularly need to travel up and down to see them. You may even be required to spend a few nights in nearby hotels.

Not all of these will be exotic locations mind you, and in fact, some can be … let's say … unglamorous … but one thing is for sure: you'll never be stuck in the same office from 9–5.

As well as travelling around the country, you may occasionally get to travel on international projects. Naturally, the travel and all your expenses when away from home are paid for by your firm, so it's quite liberating to put all your expenses on your company card and not pay a penny for time away from home. Obviously, this has to be reasonable – you can't go on shopping sprees or dine in the finest restaurants (at least not too often!)

15

Throughout all your travels, along the way, you will have the opportunity to meet exciting people, broaden your network and develop contacts across the globe.

7. Great working conditions

Consulting firms recognise that people and the expertise that they bring are their biggest assets. As a result, everything they do is geared towards helping you perform optimally.

If you work late, you'll get dinner paid and a cab home. If your laptop melts down, you'll get a new one couriered to you. If something in your personal life comes up, you can rearrange things and take time off the very next day, as long as the work is covered or there is no upcoming deadline.

In the same way, if your day involves a few calls and the reviewing or preparing of documents, many firms are very happy for you to work from home. You can dial into meetings or use videoconferencing - just make sure that you've changed out of your pyjamas for at least the top half!

The fact that you are treated as an adult who can take complete responsibility for your own work is such a refreshing change, and in my estimation, one of the greatest perks of the job.

One more thing I'll mention here: no nights or weekends. This is HUGE and should not be underestimated. No more having to check your on-call rota for social events and no more missed weddings, sports matches, AA meetings, or anything else you've been missing out on.

8. The money and job prospects

There are very few careers where you can see a roadmap to true financial wealth.

The starting salary for an entry-level management consultant is around £30K. These posts are usually filled by graduates straight from university. After a couple of years this can quickly rise to anywhere between £40K and £50K. After another two or three years, a 'manager level' management consultant (equivalent to a junior registrar and with similar responsibility in terms of managing a team) can earn upwards of £65K. Senior managers often earn upwards of £85K. This will be discussed further in Chapter 3, where I have described the different entry points for medics.

If you make it to the top as a partner, you could be earning hundreds of thousands of pounds per year and will truly be among the world's elite. Salaries close to half a million or one million are not unheard of, depending on the firm and individual performance.

Be prepared to work very, very hard to get there, as there will be more than a little competition along the way. However, if you are successful, the possibilities are endless ...

What I will miss about a medical career

- The kudos
- That satisfaction of doing good
- The camaraderie of the staff

17

- Wearing scrubs
- The simple gratitude from patients

What I will not miss

- Hospital politics
- Canteen food
- Interspecialty fighting and turf wars
- Selling your soul just to do what's best for patients (i.e. pleading for imaging / more time from A&E / urgent theatre slots / referrals)
- Going home mentally and physically broken some days
- Sometimes feeling unsupported by your own team or seniors
- Fixed leave
- The pay

If these sound like reasons that make YOU want to go into consulting, then read on! In the next chapter, we explore the top reasons why people fall at the first hurdle ...

Chapter 2

Seven reasons why doctors fail to become management consultants

1. They lack the guts to do it

Many doctors consider management consulting. It may be considered one of the holy grails of alternative careers, along with banking or any non-specific general job 'in the city', which some pundits seem to refer to. It's probably due to the transferable skills that we have as medics, as well as our proven academic achievements.

There will be some medics that decide that it's not the right thing for them, and in those cases, dismissing it as a career choice is absolutely the right thing to do. It's not all things to all people, and certainly you could become disillusioned if you go into it for the wrong reasons. However, if it is something that strongly appeals to you, go forth with confidence.

Bearing this in mind, many of those who *do* want to go into consulting never end up doing a single thing about it. Why?

They are afraid of stepping out of their comfort zone. They are afraid of rejection. Or, maybe, they are afraid of the mammoth effort needed to begin this new endeavor. If you are in any of these categories, I don't blame you. Medicine is a job that drains us both physically and mentally, and you really need to want to get into consulting in order to make that change.

Taking the plunge into the unknown comes naturally for a very small number of people. If you are one of them – congratulations. For the rest of us, how do we mitigate the fear of taking a step towards something we can't see or feel?

It's really simple: have the self-belief to do it, and find out as much about it as possible. In other words – do your research. The more you find out about it, the less of an unknown it becomes, and the easier it seems to be. This growing awareness leads neatly onto my next point.

2. They don't do their research about the job

This is a critical and highly underestimated part of the process. Without knowing what you might be doing, the where and why, the selection panel will see right through you.

Let's say you want to become a surgeon. Would you turn up to an interview without having some idea of the sub-specialty you want to go into, or without ever having set foot in an operating theatre or seen an incision being made? I didn't think so.

Be prepared to answer the following questions thoroughly as you face that selection panel:

- What is management consultancy?
- What kind of work will I be doing?
- Where will I be working?
- Who will I work with?
- What is the working life like?
- What will I be expected to deliver?
- How can I succeed in this career?

21

How will you answer these questions? Your responses can come through a variety of avenues:

- Finish this book!
- Reading articles about consulting (try to understand the pros and cons).
- Consulting firms' own websites & recruitment evenings or events where you can speak to the firm's recruitment reps.
- Specialist Internet sites designed to prepare you for consulting, e.g. management- consulted.com or caseinterview.com.
- Talk to people you know in consulting firms or find someone who knows a management consultant!
- Read publications related to management consulting and business; e.g. if it's healthcare consulting in the UK you are interested in, read the HSJ so you understand the climate.
- Other things to read could be the Wall Street Journal, The Economist, The FT, etc.

3. They apply to the wrong firm at the wrong time

Making this error is akin to trying to go on holiday by packing your bags, getting your passport ready, but arriving at the wrong airport terminal two hours late or two weeks early because you heard some aeroplanes were departing, and Barbados is supposed to be nice.

- Is the firm you are applying to the right match for you, and are you a match for them?
- Are they hiring?

If you can answer yes to these two questions, this will dramatically increase your chances of success.

How do you go about answering the first question? Simple - by doing your research on the company website and talking to people who work there. There is no other way around this. You will glean many subtle nuances from talking to someone about the company's culture and how they work, which will make you seem so much more prepared, You will also have a better idea of whether you'll fit into the firm and enjoy working there.

As for the second question, find out if they are advertising. For example, LinkedIn is a good hiring indicator (I will say more about LinkedIn later). Are they actively advertising elsewhere or going to university management societies with stands at recruitment fairs? Does their name come up in job or recruitment articles or supplements? If they are showing signs of 'being out there' or of having activity in public events, chances are they might be recruiting. If they need people, you have an infinitely higher chance of getting your foot through the door.

The only caveat is that the popular consulting firms may not be advertising, as they are always inundated with applicants. Talk to someone you know there. If you don't know anybody, look on the 'jobs' section of the firm's website to find names and contact them.

What you don't want to do is apply to a firm that isn't recruiting at all. As a working doctor you have finite time. You don't want to waste time or become disillusioned by trying to go somewhere you can't – find an alternative. If it's not sunny in Barbados, there's always California!

4. They fail to demonstrate that they have relevant experience or tailor their CV

How can we as medics, who have usually never done any formal consulting, demonstrate sufficient experience in the field? Well, whilst we may not be able to show true consulting experience, we can show relevant skills and attributes that are relevant to consulting. Go back through your CV and pick out things such as the following:

- Teamworking.
- Leading a team.
- Problem solving.
- Taking initiative.
- Project management.
- Staying calm under pressure and working to a deadline.
- Financial analysis and saving money / turning a profit.
- Presenting to a small or large audience.
- Inspiring and motivating change.

24

- Strong skills in Microsoft Word, Excel and PowerPoint.
- The ability to sit down for long periods of time and concentrate.

Although this list is not exhaustive, it is a great place to start. I personally rely on these skills almost every day in the management consulting world. You may not have all of these but I am willing to bet that you have done audits, small quality improvement projects, academic work, fundraising events or something else where you have really made a difference.

For example, you may have saved a hospital department tens of thousands of pounds; you may have shown a team of 20 people how to work differently and saved them time; or kept a long project running to time (tell them how you did it, how you kept track of it and how you motivated the team). Alternatively, you may have produced a complex piece of analysis or writing that was well received, and furthermore, tell them how you collaborated with others. In consulting, we create lengthy documents all the time for clients and often revise them multiple times with input from various people on the team.

If your working career is too short and you don't have any of these experiences, then think back to what you did in medical school. If you don't have anything at all, then get cracking with involvement in relevant projects that you can use to demonstrate your dedication and talents.

25

5. Their communication skills let them down

Doctors are great communicators. We can explain complex things clearly to people, no matter what their academic background is. We can break bad news and convince people it's the best thing ever. We can convince our radiology colleagues to do urgent scans in the middle of the night. We can gain consent from a parent for operating on their child and tell someone else that their grandfather passed away. And we can do all this at 5 a.m. on a night shift with no food, water or sleep. So how could our communication skills possibly let us down?

In a word: attitude.

Some medics try to get into consultancy purely on their status or a sense of entitlement. Recruiters dislike arrogance. It is an obvious and unattractive trait that makes for a difficult colleague and an awkward interview.

Simply being a medic does not bestow you with the right to automatically enter management consultancy. People want to know that you are personable, approachable and can hold a conversation on any level. After all, the success of most projects and certainly the chance of you getting called for repeat work (and therefore bringing funds into the organisation) depends entirely on how you communicate with your clients and the relationships you build with them.

26

It's not just about clients either. If you're going to be in an office for weeks on end with colleagues in a small team, they want to know that you are not going to rub anyone up the wrong way.

So how can you communicate in the right way? It's not easy. You have to score points in the interview and blow your own trumpet (something which medics are not used to) whilst at the same time coming across as easy going: Driven yet approachable. Highly skilled yet open minded. It's a delicate balance. Also, one size does not fit all as interviewers will have their own personality and will be looking for people that they can relate to. The best option, corny though it sounds, is to relax and be comfortable in your own skin. Be the best you that you can be: happy, relaxed and well-mannered, and your attitude and communication skills will shine through.

6. They underperform on the technical aspects of the interview

You could have done all the research in the world, be the best communicator there is, but underperform on parts of the interview where they are trying to figure out your core skills.

This could be about solving a problem, doing a small presentation, being asked to talk through a complex issue or completing some mathematical tests. Again this will be highly dependent on the firm that you apply to, and you will need to prepare accordingly with careful research or by talking to people at that firm.

When talking through things, remember to make logical arguments, speak clearly and concisely, and finish with a conclusion or recommendation. Be sure to answer the question asked but add value to your answer. As for the mathematical tests, show clear reasoning and your work on the necessary steps.

The interview will be explored in greater detail in a later chapter.

7. They fail to communicate their absolute commitment and passion to changing career

Remember when applying to medical school you agonised over 'Why medicine?'. Now you have the joy of agonising over the reverse 'Why leave medicine?!'

They will certainly want to know, not only why, but also how sure you are about making your decision.

When talking about your reasons for leaving, there will be 'push' and 'pull' factors. Don't dwell on the push factors – you don't want to be seen as another disillusioned medic and no one likes a complainer.

Wait – what's that I hear you say? You *are* another disillusioned medic? You feel depressed and need to get out? You'll take any job (so long as it's lucrative)? You under-researched consulting and don't have a clue about it, but you're still the best for the job as you have 'good communication skills' and you've 'been around hospitals'. Newsflash: you cannot tell them this!

You should never lie, but you should keep the push factors to a minimum and emphasise the pull factors. It's all about the way you phrase things.

Pull factors may include the following:

- Having the opportunity to solve problems on a larger scale.
- Having the time and space to get into the detail of what is really going on in an organisation.
- Suggesting changes for the better in organisations (though you may not be around long enough to see the effects of your changes).
- Working with a variety of different organisations and learning from them.
- Developing strong relationships with clients and helping them in any way needed.
- Working with intelligent and interesting colleagues from different backgrounds to challenge the way you think (this is something I have certainly enjoyed).
- The chance to use some creativity.
- Seeing how the world really works and thinking laterally about new ways of doing things.

Remember to personalise your motivations and put a little bit of 'you' into everything – this makes it easier to talk and your passion will shine through. What is it about your current job

29

that you find the most enjoyable or what is it that you do in your life that brings you the most joy? Can you draw some parallels from your life with consulting that are a really big pull factor?

For example in your current job, if you really enjoy the doctor-patient relationship, you can say you're really going to love building relationships with clients and helping them through difficult projects. If you love sorting out problems on the wards with the way things happen or the way people do things, emphasise how you love to solve practical problems. If you loved doing your academic research and presenting it, tell them that you really enjoy putting time and care into researching the finer details and relish the challenge of writing detailed, structured and coherent arguments.

Upon reflection, I see that I've used the word 'love' here quite a lot without even realising it. This word tends to creep in when you're passionate about something. Remember to convey some of that enthusiasm.

Chapter 3

Life as a management consultant: salary, lifestyle & a typical week

So we've danced around the topic of the perks of the job and why people don't get into consultancy, but let's get into the nitty gritty. Let's learn a little about the industry, the career ladder and more about the job. But first, story time ...

Case study: a day in the life of a management consultant

Coffee. Always start the day with the right wake up call. Something rich, dark and smooth will be just right.

Inevitably you will have checked your phone by 8 a.m to see whether there is a meeting or if a client needs something urgently. You'll arrive shortly before 9 a.m. to catch up with pressing emails and to check the day's schedule before sitting down with the team for an hour to learn about the project's progress. Another cup of coffee.

You might have a team brainstorming session or reflect on a particularly challenging issue, and then head off to a briefing with the clients. You'll share some data ahead of the early afternoon presentation and make some tweaks to the PowerPoint before a heading back to the office to put the presentation together with the team.

A conference call at lunch is not ideal as you have so much to cram in, but you switch the video off and get on with other tasks while keeping one ear on the call.

You grab a sandwich from Pret on your way to the boardroom but decide against eating it as the CEO is there and you don't want crumbs everywhere. The presentation goes well. There are some difficult questions, but the partner on the project chimes in to save the day. You dial a cab and make a mad dash to the station in time for a train to an evening meeting, downing a quick coffee on the train to recharge.

Once done, you head home and perch on your bed with your laptop. Just a few more excel sheets to crunch through ahead of tomorrow. Hmmm. What's for dinner? Damn – didn't have lunch! Hands are trembling from the excess coffee. The Pret sandwich still looks edible. You sink your teeth into it and you get a call from an unknown number. It could be your boss or your client. Do you answer?

What is management consultancy officially?

The term management consultancy covers a wide spectrum of what is known as 'professional services'. As a management consultant, clients will hire the services of you and your firm to analyse how effectively their business is running. They might ask you to solve a particular problem, oversee a specific task or project, or give advice and recommendations on how to improve.

What kinds of projects are there?

Projects vary in size, task and duration, and they can include the following:

- Implementing a large infrastructure program.
- Cost analysis and optimisation (this usually means cutting costs!).
- Looking at staff working practices and making them more efficient.
- Streamlining pathways.
- Overseeing mergers and acquisitions of organisations.
- Developing IT solutions.
- Helping draft policy.
- Drafting applications or lengthy documents for regulatory purposes.
- General project management.
- Bid development (internal work where you support your own firm to win a project with a client).

These sorts of projects can be both health related or non-health related, depending on whether you join a firm that practices in the healthcare space or not.

How does staffing of projects work?

When you join the firm, you are effectively going into a 'pool' of talent that can be allocated to different projects. There will be a resourcing or project coordinator who looks at all the projects that have been won (yes, work doesn't grow on trees; the firm has to compete against others to win it) and who is available to staff them. If you are not actively working on a project, possess the right skills and are available to join, you will be grouped together with five or six others and sent to work on that endeavour.

In practice you don't always get much of a say in where you end up working as you are there to fulfill a need, but a good firm will try to take into account your preferences. As you rise through the ranks of the firm, you may generate your own work for the firm, and if you bring in income, you will have more of a say in how and where you work.

A project could last anywhere from six weeks to three months or in some cases twelve to eighteen months or more. More often than not, you will be on a project for a few months with one team, and then roll off onto another project with a completely new team.

As medics, we are used to locumming or changing specialty every few months, so quickly adapting to new projects or environments is very easily handled. Often in the medical or surgical world, when working in teams you have a consultant, a registrar, and a few juniors who do the bulk of the work. In the consulting world there is a similar parallel as you usually have a partner, a senior manager and a few juniors who will do the work. Consulting can be just as hierarchical as the medical world despite their best efforts to deny it!

What's the career ladder like and the salary?

Now here's the interesting bit. In the medical world, you start off as a foundation doctor or 'house officer' and work your way up through the ranks to become a consultant. In the consulting world, you start off as a consultant! You then rise up through the ranks to become a partner (Figure 1).

Just to confuse matters, some consulting firms refer to consultants as 'associates'. There can also be a step below consultant called an 'analyst' or 'intern', which is the entry point for someone just graduating from university.

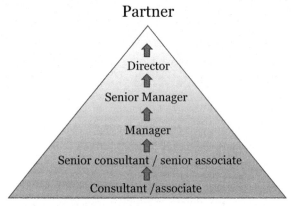

Figure 1. Consultancy Career Structure

As for the salary, here is a **very** rough salary guide for UK consulting salaries:

> Intern / analyst: starting around £26,000
>
> Consultant: £33,000–£37,000
>
> Senior consultant: £45,000–£55,000
>
> Manager: £65,000–£80,000
>
> Senior Manager: £85,000–£95,000
>
> Director: £120,000+
>
> Partner: £200,000+

Do note that each job offer will be highly individualised and salaries will vary from firm to firm, so please use these as ball-park figures and consult websites for up-to-date salaries. Managers and above will be also be offered a company car or money towards one, as well as other perks such as private healthcare.

Partners can sometimes be enrolled in profit shares on projects, so reaching half a million or more per annum is not unheard of. I can almost hear you sigh as you read this. How can a job with no nights or weekends pay so much compared to medical salaries? Well, that is what the industry pays and that is how they recruit and retain the best. Also, there can be long hours and travelling, which can lead to entire weeks or months away from home, and this needs to be offset by looking after employees.

What do you actually do on a day-to-day basis?

On a macro level, all projects have a rough structure which builds on the following:

1. Identify a potential project and apply (this may be a competitive process with other firms or a unique opportunity identified from an existing relationship).
2. If the 'bid' has been successful, meet with the client to identify their requirements and the scope of the work.
3. Establish relationships with staff from the organisation.
4. Gather data – both quantitative and qualitative.
5. Analysis of the data.
6. Preliminary discussions with the client about early findings of data and to explore potential solutions.
7. Test solutions and gather further supplementary data.
8. Finalise findings and present options to the client with the recommended course of action.

This process can take weeks or months, and occasionally you may be involved in a project that doesn't quite fit the structure above or they wish for you to provide project management support rather than provide a particular solution.

On a micro level, as a general rule of thumb, teams spend Monday to Thursday on a 'client site', i.e. actually working with the organisation, sitting in their offices and interacting closely with the staff. Your days will be a mixture of the following activities:

- Team meetings.
- Trying to organise meetings with clients.
- Actually having meetings with clients.
- Waiting around for meetings with clients.
- Rescheduling client meetings that have been cancelled.
- Trying to match up multiple people's diaries to have more meetings.
- Having conference calls (a virtual meeting).
- Having catch-ups over coffee (which is also a kind of meeting).
- Travelling to meetings or running in between them.
- Also, if you're lucky, some time alone to get some work done!

On Fridays, there is the unwritten law of coming back to the main office. This has the following effect:

- Fridays are a good day to schedule collaborative meetings with your colleagues or for generally catching up with what's going on in the sector.
- If you arrive in the office at 9.01a.m. on a Friday, you won't get a desk (it's all about hot-desking).

39

- If you've been slogging your guts out all week, **Friday is POET's day** (if you don't know what that means, I suggest you Google it).

Consulting is a career that is as much about people as it is about data and process. All meetings serve a distinct purpose. The team meetings, for example, are vital to set the tone of the project, to set clear goals and timelines, and to help everyone else see what others are doing. They also help the team to bond, to share experiences of the client and to come up with ideas and strategies to overcome challenges.

Client meetings depend on the stage of the project and they can be about establishing the scope of the work, revealing early findings or putting forward some recommendations. They may even be about sharing current progress with the client, whilst gently dropping in some ideas for further work.

At the end of the day, what are my outputs?

In medicine, our aim is to make patients better by identifying the cause of pain or illness and giving them advice or recommending treatments to relieve their discomfort. Consulting is not so different. The purpose of the job is to make organisations better by identifying the causes of their problems and giving advice and suggestions to improve them.

But what are our tangible outputs?

As management consultants, in terms of tangible 'products' of work, we produce mainly the following:

- PowerPoint presentations.
- Emails.
- Word documents.
- Excel documents.
- If you are lucky, some software.
- Positive results in the organisation of your client (if all goes well).

Do consider the following aspect of the job carefully. PowerPoint presentations, or 'decks' as they are referred to in the industry, are at the top of the list because they are the most frequent. I will say this again for emphasis: you will spend hours and hours of your life making PowerPoint presentations. You will spend much of your day shifting text boxes, adjusting font sizes and rearranging slides. You'll invariably always use the same corporate template, so you don't even get to play around with the different slide themes!

Once again, take a step back and take note of this. In medicine, we directly help people, see them smile, get a thank you, and see a life changed for the better. Some people feel that the rewards in consulting are nowhere near as great. You will spend most of your life as a management consultant, sitting in meetings, travelling to them or making PowerPoint presentations. Don't say you haven't been warned.

How will you be assessed?

You may have thought your royal college endorsed eportfolio was bad enough. You joined consultancy and were glad to see the back of that. However, to your horror, they have similar online eportfolios! So welcome back to logging in, writing a personal development plan, choosing your competencies that you want to work towards, and recording feedback and progress updates along the way.

Why? Due to their vast number of employees, they need to automate the process of recording development goals, 360-degree feedback and all the other joyous tasks we do. So, unfortunately, there is no escaping this.

Having said that, as medics, we are used to jumping through hoops and filling in online forms, so more of the same is not too taxing. It's a necessary evil, and it's the tool that will be used to monitor and observe your 'progress'. This may vary, however, in smaller 'boutique' consulting firms.

How do you get promoted?

This depends on your seniority and the firm you are in. Usually, it takes around 2–3 years at a particular level before you can progress but occasionally slightly longer or slightly quicker. Unlike our medical careers, there is no automatic, time-based progression.

As with everything in your working life, you are constantly being watched. Other criteria that be used in assessing your suitability for progression include the following:

- The quality of your work and presentations.
- The strength of your interactions with clients and colleagues.
- Discussions with your mentor or 'supervisor' within the firm.
- Impressions that senior managers, directors and partners have of you.
- The 'extra-curricular' internal work you have done for the firm in terms of internal roles, organising conferences or educational sessions.
- Your chargeability – how much billable work you are doing for clients and, therefore, how much money you are bringing into the firm.
- Any new work you have secured – again this is about how much money you have made the firm.

Remember that consulting is a pyramidal structure, so competition at each step is fierce – much more so than in medicine. Be prepared to work hard, to go beyond normal working hours to get noticed and to network within the firm. It is not an easy ride, and because you are a medic, you will not get treated any differently. It may get you through the interview, but once you're there, you're expected to work and perform as well as anyone else.

Some final facts to ponder

- Starting out in consulting is like starting out as a house officer: you have to learn the ropes, do the dirty work and the hours can be long.
- You need to be proactive and take control of your own career once you are in a firm.
- You may have heard of the up or out culture: if you fail to get promoted in a few years or you have failed to make an impression, you tend to get sidelined and eventually you may have to leave the firm.
- Consulting careers can be less secure and highly dependent on the market. There may be a growth phase where firms are hiring heavily or a shrinking phase where firms are trying to streamline and reduce staff.
- It will take time and effort to progress but the rewards could be massive.
- Job satisfaction differs from medicine and it needs to be right for you.

Chapter 4

Preparing to become a management consultant

Your preparation and route into consulting largely depends on what stage of your career you are at and how much previous experience you have.

There are two main points of entry:

1. Graduate Entry, e.g. medical student / foundation doctor.
2. Experienced hire, e.g. specialist trainee or consultant level and above.

There is a grey area where if you have just completed foundation training or are an early specialist trainee, you may feel more senior than the typical graduate entrants but do not quite match the criteria for an experienced hire. In this case, it depends on the level of consulting knowledge and experience you have, and the number and quality of projects you have been involved in.

Graduate entry

A word of warning for medical students

When medical students ask me about getting into consultancy without completing their degree or at least having worked as a doctor, I worry. Why? Well, if you complete your course, you have infinitely more options open to you than if you just leave halfway. If you quit early, you have nothing to show for all that work, no degree and many years of hard work wasted. Worst of all, you're just the same as everybody else. No advantages.

If you graduate, at least you're a doctor and no one can ever take that away from you. It will always be an ace in your deck and will look great on your CV or on your driving license.

Please bear in mind, that this is just one way of looking at things. There will be people who have every right to disagree with me as there have been many medical students who went straight into consulting. They were sure about what they wanted to do and probably did not enjoy medicine, but I can't help feeling that, sadly, they will forever have a huge hole in their life experience.

How foundation training prepares you for consulting

Should you complete foundation training, too? My strong recommendation is that you should complete this, get your degree and work for two years as a doctor. Why? Well, it goes back to experience.

There are two good reasons why finishing foundation training will make you better all round:

> 1. Life skills – Being a junior doctor is one of the most challenging times of your life. Your time management skills, your physical and emotional resilience, your confidence, your communication skills, your take on life, your ability to multitask and prioritise ... the list goes on and all of these will be tested and trained on a daily

47

basis. These two years will be the best training for anything life throws at you. It changes you for the better in a way you'll never imagine. Those who have been through it, underestimate how valuable a time it is in their life. It is hard work, but also immensely rewarding if you can see past the daily grind.

Completing your foundation training is probably the most valuable thing you'll ever do and better than any leadership skills course or life skills course you would pay money for. Think of it as a two-year immersive training program where you get molded into a lean, mean, efficient version of yourself. You will be a lot more employable than simply as a medical student.

2. Understanding healthcare better – If you are truly serious about consulting, and healthcare is what you want to specialise in, then having worked in the field will give you so much more empathy and understanding about what goes on in a hospital.

Tips on preparing for consulting at graduate entry

Every time you are in hospital, you need to go about your work or training with your eyes open and try to answer the following questions and do these things:

- How do the departments run? Analyse them in detail.
- What budgetary constraints are there and what decisions are they making?
- What pressures are there on staffing and other resources?
- Meet your managers.
- Go to departmental and board meetings.
- Get involved with quality improvement projects.

The majority of your preparation at this stage will be around your CV and interview, where you will need to talk about your experience and describe your motivation for the career change. More information on these topics can be found in chapters 6–7. Some of the advice for experienced hires in the next section may also apply to you, so don't skip it!

Experienced Hires

This is the second entry point for consulting that comes later in your career. Arguably you are at your most useful at this stage. Within the NHS, you are now a decision maker and can take responsibility. Outside the NHS you are a highly valuable resource who comes with all the amazing skills of a doctor, exemplifying confidence, the ability to learn, the energy and the drive to succeed. You'll also have a much more rounded view of the world, and your experience will mean people might even listen to what you have to say.

How does your preparation differ from the previous section?

> 1. Your reasons for leaving must be even clearer (again, remember to talk about pull factors rather than push factors).
> 2. The experience you have must be even more significant.

It's no longer enough to have 'been involved' with 'stuff'. How did you make it happen? Was it your idea? What made you think of 'genius plan X' to solve 'major NHS flaw No. #47395'? How did you save millions of pounds or how did you reduce the inpatient length of stay to minus one?

Be bold with your statements and achievements, and be able to back them up. As medics, we are terrific at underselling ourselves and that's not a particularly positive trait.

Tips on applying for consulting as an experienced hire:

- Understand the current climate of the NHS (not just contracts but everything from commissioning to the transatlantic trade and investment partnership for example).
- Brush up on the existing NHS structures and the myriad of organisations that influence different aspects of it.
- Go to a CCG meeting.
- Attend departmental or CEO board meetings.
- Know your own trust inside out (read the minutes on the intranet) and understand the key issues – go to the managers and talk to them.
- Know the cost pressures that your own department is under. How much money does your specialty bring in per activity?
- Above all, what have you done about all of these?
- How can you demonstrate initiative and leadership?

You are more senior than a new graduate, and, therefore, you will be expected to know more about the inner workings of the NHS and the financial, political and clinical drivers of change.

Other preparation for experienced hires

In your preparation, you need to reframe any projects that you've worked on, in a light that reflects your ability to identify problems, analyse them, solve them and make change happen in a lasting way with significant gains and

51

improvements. Don't forget to mention negotiation skills or your familiarity with best practice and quality improvement projects.

In addition, you need to highlight the following attributes in particular:

- Open mindedness
- Adaptability
- Clear career plans
- Thought leadership
- Strong and proven experience in leading change
- Authoritativeness yet approachability

The first two on the list are critical, as you need to be able to learn, be receptive to new ways of thinking and be able to change your style to a new career in consulting.

Career planning for experienced hires

As for career plans, you need to be very clear about how you came to this decision, how everything you've done up to now has led to this (through either excellent planning or sheer accident) and where you are going. Is consultancy an 'add-on career' for you? Or is it going to be your main income? What are your salary expectations? Can you potentially afford a pay cut or would you be willing to take one just to get into the field or do you want equal or better remuneration for changing careers (in which the case for recruiting you has to be that much more watertight).

If you have been a consultant or GP for a few years and brought about real change in a specialty, perhaps across several trusts or at the CCG or national level, then you may be eligible to become a 'subject matter expert' or SME. You might be paid for your advice and expertise on an ad-hoc basis but arrangements vary by firm.

Thought leadership is way of demonstrating your interest and expertise in a subject. It also demonstrates that you have the discipline to write and the ability to articulate clearly.

State your experience in leading change. This is how you can really single yourself out as an individual that the firm cannot afford to pass on! Be descriptive in what you've done, the bigger and more impactful the change the better. But even smaller projects can be valuable if you demonstrate leadership and a methodical approach to tackling a problem.

As for authoritativeness yet approachability – are you extremely knowledgeable and respected but at the same time down to earth and able to hold a conversation with just about anyone? As I've alluded to before, arrogance is an unattractive trait. Confidence on the other hand is highly valued. Sometimes the line between these two traits can get blurred, so be aware how you present yourself.

Starting conversations early as an experienced hire

There is one final thing to touch on as an experienced hire, i.e. starting conversations early. You can't blindly send in an application without discussion. Talk to recruiters six months to a year ahead of your intended change over, and ask about opportunities and what they are looking for.

It's entirely reasonable to explore time commitments and salary expectations. You are in charge of your own life after all, and it's better that both parties are up front. If you can get to know their requirements and what positions they have available, you can make meaningful decisions about what you might do or how you can contribute, without the actual pressure of a job interview. Don't be afraid to highlight your skills and ask for genuine feedback about how you can increase your chances of success. These discussions will only show that you are open and honest.

If your skill set matches what the firm does or needs, even if there isn't a formal job available, they could create a role for you if they like and value you. But these things are time consuming (i.e. behind the scenes discussions and authorizations, etc.), which is why it's worth having the conversations early.

Preparatory courses such as 'How to get into Management Consultancy for Medics' has course tutors who have successfully transitioned from Medicine to Management Consultancy. These experts are there to share ALL the insider info, professional tips and advice on how to succeed. The course gives a great introduction to what management consulting is, gives you the opportunity to work on a 'real life' case study that you may be faced with at work, and provides in depth CV and interview preparation sessions. Find out more at www.eurekadoc.com/courses.

Chapter 5

Where to apply & how to apply

The types of management consultancy firms

Not all management consultancy firms are created equally. Broadly, they can fit into three categories:

1. Dedicated large management consultancy firms. The three most prestigious firms are referred to as the '**Big Three**': McKinsey, BCG, and Bain.
2. Consultancy arms of audit firms or other firms, e.g. KPMG, EY, PWC and Deloitte (note that these four in particular are known as the '**Big Four**' audit firms).
3. Boutique or smaller independent consultancy firms.

What is the difference between the various types of firms?

The firms may differ in several ways, but below are some of the key areas of difference you should consider when applying:

- Size
- Nature of work
- Brand / reputation
- Company culture

The large and independent firms are reliant solely on their consultancy skills as they have no other source of income.

57

Their survival, therefore, relies on their reputation and ability to deliver high-quality services that clients will turn to again and again. They will hire the very best, are challenging to get into and will work you hard.

Outside of clinical practice, auditing refers to the the mandatory process by which companies have to get their accounting processes checked by a recognised firm. Audit firms often expand from providing traditional accountancy services to include an additional advisory role or consultancy arm of their business. These firms will be huge and will have invested a great deal in looking after their employees. They are more likely to have a reasonable work-life balance though you will still be expected to work hard.

The smaller firms will typically have been set up in the last few years by a fewer number of partners. The team size will be quite small, and you will have constant interaction with the senior members and partners of the team. Again you will have to work very hard. Also, because you may be in much closer proximity to your colleagues than with any of the other firms, it is vital for both and your firm that you fit in to the culture of that firm. Their employee benefits scheme may not be as well established as larger firms, but what you may get back in terms of mentorship will more than make up for this.

Where to look for jobs

Websites

By far and away, this is the easiest and most obvious way to look for a job. Make a list of the consultancy firms that you want to apply to. Bookmark their recruitment page (usually under 'opportunities', 'careers' or 'join the team') and on a regular basis, check through all the jobs they have available. Don't forget to use the filtering system so that you can narrow down the searches.

Once you find a job that you like, upload your CV and hit apply.

LinkedIn

If you are not on LinkedIn, technically you don't exist. It is a professional network that you have to join if you are serious about getting your name out there. What's more, you can follow news about companies you wish to apply for as well as search the jobs section. Many consultancy firms advertise their roles via LinkedIn, and so this is a critical job-hunting resource you don't want to miss out on.

Recruiters

You can find a recruitment agency that specialises in consultancy or if you join LinkedIn, they will find you. The benefit of sharing your details with them is that they can do a lot of the legwork for you, as they will have up-to-date information on who is recruiting, and they can even prep you a little on what the companies are like before interviews.

Recruitment fairs

This is a great opportunity to get up close and personal with current employees of the firms themselves. Not only are they signaling their intent to recruit, they are ready and willing to answer any questions you have about working for the firm. This really is your opportunity to ask anything you like without the pressure of the interview situation. If you like the sound of what you hear, have a casual chat about why you think you may be suitable for the job, and why you are interested in them. After the chat, exchange details with them and find out how to apply.

Friends and colleagues

If you have this route available to you, this is probably the best way to go about finding jobs. People working at the firm will often be the first to know about potential plans to expand the team or about posts opening up. Check in with them from time-to-time and find out about those jobs that aren't advertised or get filled up before they are.

If you don't know anyone directly, ask around. You'll be surprised about how many people know someone who works in consultancy, and you can glean a great deal of information from them.

How to apply

This is very straightforward. If you have been recommended or referred in by a friend or colleague, then they will ask for your CV electronically. Do not voluntarily force your CV onto people if they haven't asked. They will most likely be too busy and won't be interested or pleased.

If you are applying directly, the firm will usually direct you to a portal on their website. If you go via a recruiter, as with a friend or colleague, again simply pass on your CV.

Chapter 6

Scoring criteria for the application process

The process begins right from the moment you fill in the online form or send in your CV. Everything from that moment onwards counts towards your success.

Whether it's your CV or your application form, there are some key domains that you will be scored in. The exact 'scoring' may vary from firm to firm. Some may allocate points whereas others may take a general overview and make a judgment call about suitability for interview shortlisting. There is no uniform process; however, these are the domains that your application will be judged on:

- Presentation
- Technical accuracy
- Brevity
- Experience
- Competence
- Adding value

Presentation

Do you have an eye for simplicity, clarity and general aesthetics? Does your application look nice? Does it read well? Not too cramped and not too spaced out.

More importantly, if you were producing a document to the same standard for a client who was 'paying' you for your time, would your application stand up to their scrutiny or would it be an embarrassment?

Selection teams will not appreciate unreadable content and more worryingly, they may not pick up important bits of information that you are trying to convey. Spend time on the way things look. First impressions do count.

Technical Accuracy

This goes without saying. No mistakes should be made. This is an industry that prides itself on perfection and delivering high-quality output for their demanding clients. Go through your entire submission line-by-line, word-by-word, at least five times. Then get someone else to do it. Then check it again. Then come back to it another day.

On the first sweep, concentrate on checking for typos and read the words out loud. On the next sweep, look at fonts and text sizing. Then look at formatting, line spacing and so on. I won't insult your intelligence anymore, but you get the picture. You don't want your application to be buried at the bottom of the bin with yesterday's financial times and this morning's coffee cups because of one silly mistake.

Brevity

A CV should be two pages. Full stop. For medics with ten page CVs, this can be incredibly challenging. How can you describe all those jobs where you did manual evacs on geriatric wards or detail your 9th podium presentation for that bizarre case report?

Sadly, you have to be ruthless with your editing. Publications and presentations might have to be abridged in the form of two lines saying how many of each you have – perhaps with a mention of a particular highlight, which you may believe to be relevant to your career in consulting.

As for courses attended, delete them. Ouch.

Bring forward your management section and any leadership roles you have into their own section. In your employment history, highlight the key achievements from each of your posts that demonstrate how you thought through a problem and came up with a solution. Don't forget to point out the tangible benefits in terms of cost or performance, which, naturally, you had a big part to play in, at each of the places you've worked at.

If you need more help with this, try to attend one of our regular one-day courses on how to get into Management Consultancy for Medics, which includes a focused CV and interview preparation session. Register at www.eurekadoc.com/courses.

Experience

They will be looking at how many years you have worked since graduating, how far you have progressed and the nature of the roles you have undertaken.

Why? Two reasons: First, suitability for positions of responsibility, and secondly, salary. This will enable them to manage both their own and your expectations.

Someone relatively junior, who has worked only for a year or two, will certainly not be ready for a manager position and won't warrant a salary more than that of a consultant or senior consultant. Someone with many years of clinical experience and vast amounts of experience chairing meetings and leading large teams on projects is going to be undervalued if they are brought in at anything below a senior manager level.

Your experience is crucial for them to evaluate what you can do and where you might fit into the team. It is very important that you demonstrate your qualities and abilities during the recruitment process so that you get the job that you want.

Competence

Are you smart enough for the job? As a medic, your academic credentials will be more than adequate. What they need to know is whether you are dynamic enough for the job and whether you have the capability to do what is required. In other words, can you fulfill the core competencies of a management consultant?

Skills that you should be able to demonstrate that interviewers will be looking for:

- Can you write?
- Can you analyse?
- Can you break down large problems into smaller ones?
- Can you demonstrate logical reasoning?

In terms of people skills, the following are qualities that they will be looking for:

- Can you lead teams?
- Can you inspire people?
- Can you motivate and manage change?
- Are you a team worker?

Adding Value

For everything that you do or have done in your current and previous roles, not only is it important to highlight what you've done but how it added value to the organisation. Here is an example:

> 'I successfully chaired committee X for three years',

> is better written as

> 'During the three years that I chaired committee X, I increased ratings by Y, revenue by Z and secured a grant from A to keep the committee going for another five years. I did this by ...'

> Or

> 'I was head of Department M, a role that I really enjoyed because I made things better for the staff and customers',

> might be improved by

67

'In my role as head of Department M, I implemented an efficiency measure N that halved our inventory and halved our costs. I enjoyed seeing our staff work more effectively and noticed a positive change with customer satisfaction ratings: in a sample of 500 surveys, satisfaction improved from 13% very satisfied to 79% very satisfied. This meant that our department was saved from closure and became the company's second most profitable division'.

This is not dissimilar to the 'STAR' model where you have to describe the *Situation*, the *Task* or problem that needed to be tackled, the *Action* which you took, and the *Result* that came about as a result of that action.

Just remember that a list of jobs and positions is meaningless to an employer. They need it to be put in context, and they need to understand clearly what you achieved and **why your role in the job was significant to the functioning of the organisation.**

If, on paper, things come together, and you paint a clear, concise and relevant picture of how you would be suited to management consultancy, then you stand a good chance of being progressed to the next stage.

Chapter 7

The management consultancy interview & how you will be assessed

So your CV and application form did the job. Congratulations – you're in! Is it that easy? Not quite.

What happens next depends both on the firm and also on whether you are a graduate entrant or an experienced hire. Let's start with graduate entry.

Graduate Entry

Once your application goes through, you may be emailed some links to take some online tests. This is the way in which the firms weed out the weaker candidates and make their job of selection easier. It's also far more cost effective than interviewing everyone. Let's now explore the kinds of tests you might be asked to do.

Psychometric testing

This is a critical part of the process and gives your employer a very good idea of your abilities and personality. In the comfort of your own home, you will be asked to complete several timed, online tests. They will examine a number of the following areas:

- Personality
- Verbal or logical reasoning
- Non-verbal reasoning
- Numerical aptitude

There are plenty of web-based resources and examples available online, so do practice these. Some find that GMAT (entry exams for MBA candidates) preparation tests and practice papers are excellent for brushing up on the math skills needed to complete these.

When you come to do the tests, do not cheat on them or get someone else to do them for you. They will more than likely be repeated at the selection centre and significant discrepancies in scoring will signal your dishonesty.

With the personality test, there is no right or wrong answer, and it is dangerous to try and second-guess what they are looking for. They will find out your true personality in face-to-face interviews anyway, and what's more, if you are honest with who you are, you are more likely to find a job that you are suited to.

Situational judgment tests

You may also be asked to take a situational judgment test (SJT). You will be given various scenarios with options to choose from regarding the next logical step or the solution to a problem. The scenarios are designed to portray real-life scenarios that you may face and test practical thinking with perhaps a small amount of knowledge. There are a wealth of resources out there designed to help you in your decision-making process, so I would urge you to consult those.

If you pass the tests, then the next stage is the telephone interview.

Telephone interview

There are generally two types of telephone interviews: **strength based** and **competency based**. Due to the volume of graduates coming through, these interviews can sometimes be outsourced. So you may not even be talking directly to your future employers. That may or may not take some of the pressure off you, but you still need to prepare. Let's examine the components of these interviews:

Strength-based telephone interviews are looking at your personal qualities. They will ask you to describe examples of the following traits or situations that you have been involved in:

- Your strengths
- Your weaknesses
- Conflict with a team mate and how you dealt with it
- Challenges that you've overcome
- Taking initiative
- An achievement you are proud of

They may even ask you these questions indirectly. For example, 'describe how you manage your time?' could be asked as 'should there be more hours in a day?' When you are asked an open-ended or abstract question, it's important to determine which underlying attribute they are asking about, and then show examples of how you demonstrate competence or excellence in that area.

Competency-based questions are more about your skills and knowledge. For example, questions can have a broad range:

- Tell us what you understand about our practice.
- How much experience do you have writing reports?
- Give us an example of a detailed piece of analytical work you completed.
- What do you know about this industry?
- How does the banking system or the stock market work?
- What do you know about the great depression or the financial crisis?

You may note that some of these questions are quite financial sector specific. Unfortunately, coming in quite junior, you need to demonstrate a broad knowledge of all of this subject matter. After all, your application is unlikely to be sector specific unless you come in as an experienced hire.

If you perform well on the telephone interview, you may then be invited to the assessment centre.

Assessment centre

Welcome to the shiny offices of your future firm. Again, you're not quite there yet. You'll now have to get through the hurdle of the assessment centre – this may not even be in your chosen firm's offices as this too is often outsourced, but that's beside the point. Let's now explore the two or three key elements of the assessment centre:

1. Psychometrics part 2

Just when you thought you'd completed the all-you-can-eat psychometrics buffet that happened before the telephone interview, welcome to part two. The key purpose of this is not to rescore you but to check that you are the same person that did the online tests at home and that you didn't cheat or receive help whilst doing them. If you did cheat and your unaided scores this time round are now much lower, then it's goodbye. If you cheated and your unaided scores are now much higher – first, how do you explain that, and secondly, who was it that was so awful at helping you? Get rid of them!

2. Individual exercises

This is where things get exciting. For the first time, they get to see you in action. You will be given 40–45 minutes to complete a series of tasks such as the following:

- Send an email to a line manager or a colleague informing them that you are unwell.
- Write a report summarising a 12-page document, related news story and emails.
- Analyse a spreadsheet and give them some feedback around their inventory costs.

What is the basis for these tasks?

For the email task, they are trying to assess whether you are professional and personable in a medium that can often be so impersonal. Can you get your point across? How do you approach your responsibilities? Would you offer to work from home? Do you think and act like you are part of a team?

For report writing, can you summarise effectively? Can you relay findings without embellishment? Can you pick out the relevant points? And do you draw mainly from the financial report rather than the news article?

As for the analytical piece, can you go over and above picking out simple facts? Can you work out averages? Can you pick out trends? Can you offer valuable advice and insights?

Here's a golden tip for individual tasks: these tasks are about quality not quantity. The timescales are designed to make it very difficult to finish, and this is part of the test. Does your work become more slapdash towards the end? Will you sacrifice quality for a real client? The learning point here is to prioritise the tasks and ensure that the outputs are of a high quality. This is more important than finishing the task.

3. The group exercise

For this exercise, you may be put in a group of 4–6 people. Each of you may be given slightly different information, and the task at hand might be to convince the others to support your viewpoint or convince everyone to agree to the action assigned to you.

People make the mistake of believing that this exercise is about winning and may try to control the scenario or force their viewpoint onto everyone else. Naturally the observers are there to monitor your interaction with the team and determine whether you listen. They want to know that not only are you able to convince others of your standpoint, but also are you open minded enough to consider and accept others' views. The trick is to be not too quiet and not too loud, offer polite agreement or disagreement, raise questions where appropriate and make valuable points.

Consulting is about teamwork and collaboration. Make sure you demonstrate these skills. Not only that, go the extra mile: offer to be timekeeper, scribe, take the initiative and if you notice someone is being quiet, encourage them to speak.

If you get through the assessment centre and all the above mentioned tasks, you are doing well and will be rewarded with the face-to-face interviews. From that point on, the process is similar to experienced hires, so we will move onto that – just skip to the section on face-to-face interviews.

Experienced Hires

Once you have a few years of experience, you become far more valuable. As a result of this, firms will treat you with more respect.

You're going to look for a position higher up the food chain, and because there are fewer applicants for your entry level than with graduates, you will directly meet members of the team that you're likely to work with (make sure you Google them before the interview). You're also likely to be busier, so there will be fewer selection stages. Once you've passed on your CV and if they like the sound of you, the first stage is to schedule a screening telephone interview with you.

Screening interview for experienced hires

This interview will be less structured than that for graduate entry, but they will still do their best to find out about you.

They will explore the roles you have taken in your previous jobs and ask you about your responsibilities. Make sure you have on hand examples of particularly challenging situations and how you handled them.

The tone may also be quite conversational so don't be afraid of asking questions and sprinkling in some light heartedness – no more than you would with a new patient or client, but enough to show you are relaxed, human and that you would make an excellent colleague.

Finally they might wish to know what made you choose their firm or your reasons for the career move. Again, you don't want to give a well-rehearsed robot answer, so keep it conversational while making a few points.

Providing you are pleasant, polite and have clear reasons and expectations about the role you are applying for, you will then be invited for the face-to-face interviews.

The face-to-face interviews

The themes explored in the face-to-face interviews have similarities for both graduate and experienced hires so we shall consider them together. Obviously, the expected level at which you are expected to perform will vary depending on your experience.

Interview 1

This is likely to be a gentle start to the process with one or two mid- to senior-level interviewers.

Be prepared for the basic questions:

- Tell us about yourself.
- Why this firm?
- What do you know about the industry?
- Why this career move?
- Are you happy to leave your previous post?
- What transferable skills do you have from your previous job?
- Do you have a realistic idea of what you will be expected to do?
- Can you write reports?
- How do you manage your time?
- What examples of conflicts or challenges you faced in your previous job can you share to help us understand how you work as a team.
- What examples can you show to help us understand how you work by yourself.

For the last few questions, remember to use the STAR model we talked about in Chapter 6.

This early stage is also the best time for you to ask any (carefully selected and relevant) questions that you were unable to answer through your extensive research. Don't save them up for later when the stakes are higher.

Interview 2

At this stage, you may be interviewed by someone even more senior, and things may start to get a little analytical.

You may be asked to read a case study, and then talk through the key points you have picked out and discuss how you might explore them.

The interviewer may describe common scenarios that your firm may encounter such as a merger/acquisition or a large-scale change management project. They will then ask you how you would go about the process from end-to-end.

For both of these scenarios, you must structure the answer and talk through the points logically, explaining why and how you would tackle each stage.

Finally, and this is a favourite of the strategy firms, you may be asked an estimation question. What's your favourite food? (You answer Italian or Thai, of course.) How many Italian restaurants are there in London? Or how many ping-pong balls can you fit into a Boeing 747?

You will have to do these sorts of questions without a calculator, and they are testing not only your mathematical skills but also whether you can stay calm, break down a question into smaller logical problems to solve and give a reasonable answer.

For the restaurant question, you might work out how many there are in your local area, and then multiple by the number of neighbourhoods there are in each borough. Then you estimate the number of boroughs in London. Or, you might figure out the population of London, workout the probability that a certain percentage of the people will want to eat out – and then workout the number of alternate cuisines and average restaurant seating capacity to come out with some estimates. But then what about transient tourists that may need to be factored in? You can make it as simple or as complicated as you wish or as the interviewer prompts.

For the Boeing question, you might compare the size of the plane to a certain number of buses. You might know roughly how long a car is in metres, and if the bus is three car lengths long and a certain height, you can begin to work out some volumes and, once you estimate the size of one ping-pong ball, come out with an answer that, even if wildly incorrect, will at least sound plausible.

Just think logically, identify numbers that you know of or can work with and do some basic calculations. Don't forget to qualify your answers, talk about variables and state key assumptions that you have made.

Most of all, enjoy it. Think of the estimation problems as if they were those teasers on the back of cereal packets that you used to do. If you try to enjoy the process, you will be more relaxed and will perform better.

For the Big '3' strategy firms, case interview practice is a major part of the interview and significant part of your time need to be spent on preparing for this in the months leading up to this.

Interview 3

Most firms will save the final interview for a partner. This is where you really have your chance to shine. Some people find that this is easier than the analytical stage and others find it just as nerve-racking.

There is now a trend towards preparing a presentation and delivering to the partner as if they were a client, and this is something you may be asked to do. It is a fantastic way of seeing how you perform 'in real life', and it should come fairly naturally to you. If you haven't delivered many presentations before, then do rehearse with a trusted colleague beforehand or video it, to pick up body language or voice issues that you weren't aware of.

Other things you may be asked will be similar to the first interview. Why this firm? Why are you changing? Remember to talk positively. Pull factors to the new job will be viewed better than push factors from the old job.

Other than that, the partner interview can be whatever they want it to be. Many of them throw away the rulebook. Just stay relaxed, answer their questions carefully and make sure everything you say adds authenticity to who you are and makes you a more valuable person.

Finally, note that the interview structure, order in which they are conducted and formats will vary from firm to firm and over time so use this chapter as a guide rather than a strict roadmap.

Good luck!

Chapter 8

Is consultancy really right for me?

Am I doing the right thing?

Do I *really* want to give up medicine and become a management consultant?

Perhaps it's strange that in a book about getting into management consultancy for medics, I'm going to challenge you to consider whether you really should do it?

Well, that's because I feel I have a strong moral obligation to tell you the facts. No sugar coating. No dressing things up to be better than they are. I want you to make an informed decision. Who else is going to tell you the truth? I might even save you years of heartache and regret.

If you're not sure, then leave the door open. Don't shut down your hard-earned medical career completely. Find ways to keep your skills and links going. Note that you will have to demonstrate a complete commitment to any job you apply for in consultancy, so play down the fact that you are keeping the door open.

The chance to get out of your cocoon

As medics, we lead quite sheltered working lives. We are highly trained to look after patients and communicate well as teams. Part of our inherent identity is also closely linked to being a doctor. What this means is that stepping outside your comfort zone can be both a liberating and a frightening experience.

We have all grown up in the culture of healthcare institutions, and it turns out we know very little about the rest of the world. There is so much to learn in areas such as accounting, organisational behavior, corporate finance, strategy, marketing, and beyond. So for those reasons, consultancy will open your eyes and can be a welcome change in life.

The journey inside consultancy

Being a doctor certainly gets you a little extra respect within the consultancy firm, but you won't get a free ride. You are expected to perform just as well as anyone else in the firm and, because of this, you have to adapt and learn fast. On the plus side, you will become a better version of yourself.

What about identity? When I first started in management consulting, I had an identity crisis – was I now a doctor who did consulting? Was I an ex-doctor? Had I really morphed into a full-blown management consultant overnight? I now know that many medics go through this soul-searching process, and I have to say I am a lot more comfortable in my own skin for it. You change as a person and are no longer dependent on your role as a doctor to carve out your identity.

If you get into the system, it's important to try and find people you relate to, people you can trust or those who have come from a similar position. Talk to them. Learn from them. You will not be alone.

Consulting at its best

I think, that for us as medics, consulting is at its best when it aligns with our own goals in life and what we get the most satisfaction from.

If you are someone who enjoys clinical work and making a difference to people's lives, then consulting will satisfy you when you're involved in big projects with clear outcomes that have a genuine positive impact on not one but many people's lives.

If you are someone who loves planning, strategy or being creative and solving problems, then consulting will also tick those boxes for you, providing you are involved in the right projects.

As a career, the right consulting firm will look after you, and you will develop as a person and a leader. You will get the opportunity to learn from others, work with people who think differently, and your job prospects will always be stronger after a spell in consulting.

You will get some of your life back and the money to do what you wish with it; though, ultimately, this depends on how you and your firm play out the tug of war of work / life balance. All I will say is don't be a slave to the firm. Work hard, but enjoy your life too.

Consulting at its worst

As alluded to in the very first chapter, consulting is often not glamorous. Despite the shiny buildings and the legions of people clamouring to get a job at consultancy firms, you are ultimately a hamster in a wheel designed to make a profit for the firm.

There are always projects that need to be staffed, and if they need you to sift through pages of excel documents or write reams of reports and you are not on a project, then you will be assigned that task.

You will spend your working life attached to a laptop, albeit in exotic locations such as coffee shops, train stations, Premier Inns and, of course, offices full of drones staring into their laptops. Your work will be dominated by targets, sales, winning projects and delivering outcomes, so think carefully about whether this sense of competition and these financial drivers interest you.

You will miss real people. You will miss the genuine smile of a grateful patient or their relative. You will miss the awesome bunch of can-do people who may not understand how the world works, but they know how to come together as a team and bring someone back from the brink of death.

Being a management consultant at a party certainly doesn't carry the same kudos as being a doctor, so be careful what you wish for and don't follow the crowd. Do what makes you happy.

87

Concluding Thoughts

Above all, you need to figure out what you enjoy in life, and what you want to do with it. It may be that you want to leave medicine; it may be that you want to do consultancy. But those are not your only options. Think wider than that.

If you feel consultancy is a good fit for yourself – then good luck – do your research about the firms, talk to as many people as you can to find out about the firm you're applying to and the job you will be doing. Prepare hard and, above all, believe in yourself. I did it, and so can you.

Chapter 9

Final tips to help you beat
the competition

So we've talked about the job, the application process and the interview. Let us now focus on a few final things to help you succeed on your journey.

1. Talk to people

If you are keen on working at one particular firm, get in touch with those who are at the firm, those who have left the firm, or even those who have worked with the firm as clients. Once you get talking to people, you will glean so many details about their culture and working practices that you will feel right at home in the interview.

The same applies if you don't know which firm you want to apply for. By talking to as many people as you can, you'll pick up on the subtle differences between the firms and discover something that is a deal breaker or dealmaker for you.

Remember to start these conversations a minimum of six months before you wish to apply but ideally twelve months or more before, so that you know exactly where you are applying and why.

2. Join LinkedIn to expand and grow your network

We have touched on this before in Chapter 5, but you cannot underestimate the importance of this. You need to start adding people to your network. Create your brand

and your connections. It's one of the indicators of who you are in the world.

This will also help you with point number 1: you can find people you are connected to at organisations that are of interest to you. If you make contact, they will usually be interested in hearing from you.

And if that doesn't convince you, knowing that some firms hire on the basis of your network should wrap it up.

3. Apply to the right firm at the right time

Find out whether a firm is recruiting before you apply, and if the timing is not right, find out when their next planned recruiting drive is. You don't want your CV being put to the bottom of a nonexistent pile.

When you do apply, look carefully at the role and the specifications – make sure your application matches the criteria. You don't want to waste time applying for a job you don't quite measure up to. If they later release a job that is right for you, you don't want the track record of having been unsuccessful with their firm.

4. Learn about the sector you are going for

Most people in health will naturally look for healthcare-related projects. If that is the case, you need to know about the latest white papers, government policy, financial drivers and all about any top-down reorganisations (these are always going on sadly) of key structures within the healthcare system. Know what is going on in your own hospital, talk to your managers, your CEO if you can – imagine mentioning in an interview that you discussed the new models of care or restructuring clinical pathway with your hospital chief executive over coffee.

The same applies if you are applying for a completely different industry: find out all that you can about it.

5. Your CV

Be really critical, remove anything that isn't valuable, and be ruthless in your trimming. For any statements that you make, make sure they add value – what did **you** do and what was the outcome or how did it help? You need to make it punchy.

Make sure that it is well presented, with no errors and with perfect consistency in font sizing, styles, paragraph spacing and full stops.

One last thing. I would urge you to convert your CV to a PDF. It takes 30 seconds and stops recruitment teams from seeing red and green spelling / grammar mistakes on a Word doc.

6. Sell yourself at the interview

Medics are awful at self-aggrandisation. On the whole, we can be too humble about our achievements. We play down our role and tend to share credit around the team. These are great traits to have and will make you an excellent team player once you get into consulting – except the fact that those same traits might prevent you from getting in, in the first place.

You need to 'upregulate' your achievements and take the proper credit for **your** ideas and things that **you** did to make **your** projects a success.

Don't be afraid to use the word 'I'. I led ... I designed ... I analysed ... I delegated ... I oversaw ... I presented ... I came ... I saw ... I conquered.

Tell them what was so amazing about what you did. What was it that you did or what particular insight was it that you possessed that made it all happen?

Tell them about all the teams you lead. Any situation, even a crash call, can be turned into an example of how you prioritise, how you communicate effectively, perform an analysis and make quick decisions under pressure, and how you inspire others to achieve great outcomes. Throw in a fact about how you had to leave a sick patient or how one of your team members was at risk of underperforming or how you dealt caringly with the grieving relatives. Every situation has a story to tell if you frame it right and use it to present yourself in a positive light. Sounding cringeworthy? Maybe. Is everyone else doing it? Definitely. Just don't do it in your everyday life. This is the interview 'super-you'.

Be bold. If you can't even sell yourself, who else will?

7. Be positive

Believe in yourself. You have the skills, the knowledge and the brain. Everyone started out life the same way. You have every reason to get the job as anyone else and deserve to.

Tell yourself in the mirror every night two weeks before the interview that you are an amazing, well-rounded intelligent person. Look yourself in the eye and **believe it**. Every night. Do it. You have nothing to lose.

Treat yourself – buy an expensive pair of shoes, suit or tie before the interview. But do it for yourself. Make yourself like feel a million dollars and you will shine.

On the interview morning, relax your body, think positive thoughts and think about how much you love consulting: the autonomy, the chance to use your brain, the chance to shine as an individual. Imagine jumping out of that chopper and landing on that skyscraper with the golden sun glinting off your sunglasses.

94

You can do this. Over to you now. I wish you all the best ... good luck!

Evidera.
costello
Aquarius Populat'n health
Bazian

Carnall farvar

IQViA

Kantar health

ABT Assosiates

Dalberg.

The Kings fund- think tank.
NHS England.